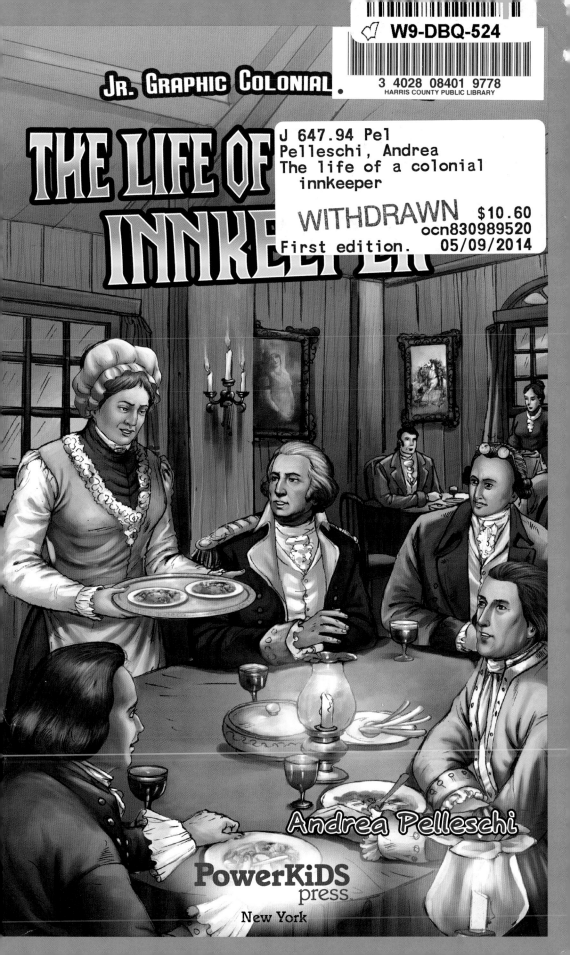

Jr. Graphic Colonial

THE LIFE OF A INNKEEPER

Andrea Pelleschi

PowerKiDS press

New York

W9-DBQ-524

3 4028 08401 9778
HARRIS COUNTY PUBLIC LIBRARY

J 647.94 Pel
Pelleschi, Andrea
The life of a colonial
innkeeper

WITHDRAWN $10.60
                ocn830989520
First edition. 05/09/2014

Published in 2014 by The Rosen Publishing Group, Inc.
29 East 21st Street, New York, NY 10010

Copyright © 2014 by The Rosen Publishing Group, Inc.

All rights reserved. No part of this book may be reproduced in any form without permission in writing from the publisher, except by a reviewer.

Note: The main characters in this book were real-life colonists who held the jobs described. In some cases, not much else is known about their lives. When necessary, we have used the best available historical scholarship on the professions and daily life in colonial America to create as full and accurate a portrayal as possible.

First Edition

Editor: Joanne Randolph
Book Design: Planman Technologies
Illustrations: Planman Technologies

Library of Congress Cataloging-in-Publication Data

Pelleschi, Andrea, 1962–
    The life of a colonial innkeeper / by Andrea Pelleschi. — First edition.
        pages cm. — (Jr. graphic colonial America)
    Includes index.
    ISBN 978-1-4777-1309-9 (library binding) — ISBN 978-1-4777-1435-5 (paperback) —
    ISBN 978-1-4777-1436-2 (6-pack)
    1. Hotelkeepers—United States—History—18th century—Juvenile literature.
    2. Hotelkeepers—United States—History—18th century—Comic books,
    strips, etc. 3. Hotelkeepers—United States—Biography—Juvenile literature.
    4. Hotelkeepers—United States—Biography—Comic books, strips, etc. 5. Campbell,
    Christiana, approximately 1723–1792—Juvenile literature. 6. Hotelkeepers—
    Virginia—Williamsburg—Biography—Juvenile literature. 7. Taverns (Inns)—
    Virginia—Williamsburg—History—18th century—Juvenile literature. 8. United
    States—History—Colonial period, ca. 1600–1775—Juvenile literature. 9. United
    States—History—Colonial period, ca. 1600-1775—Comic books, strips, etc.
    10. United States—Social life and customs—To 1775—Juvenile literature. I. Title.
    TX909.P45 2014
    647.94092—dc23
                            2012051003

Manufactured in the United States of America
CPSIA Compliance Information: Batch #S13PK1: For Further Information contact Rosen Publishing, New York, New York at 1-800-237-9932

CONTENTS

INTRODUCTION

Not only did colonial inns provide food and shelter for travelers, they were also social gathering places for **townsfolk** and places to catch up on the news of the day. Many counties required each town to have an inn. Rates had to be reasonable so middle-class travelers could afford to stay. Most innkeepers even welcomed poor families who did not have enough money to pay for a room.

MAIN CHARACTERS

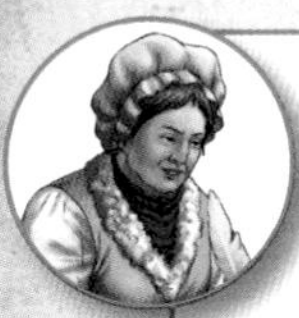

Christiana Campbell (1723–1792) Owned and operated three inns in Williamsburg, Virginia. Many famous people, including Thomas Jefferson and George Washington, frequented them.

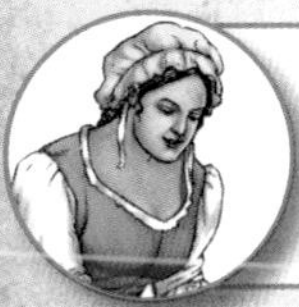

Mary "Molly" Campbell (1750–?) The older of Christiana's two daughters. She married and moved away from Williamsburg when she was 35 years old.

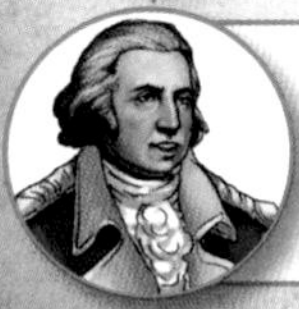

George Washington (1732–1799) Commander of American forces during the American Revolution and first president of the United States.

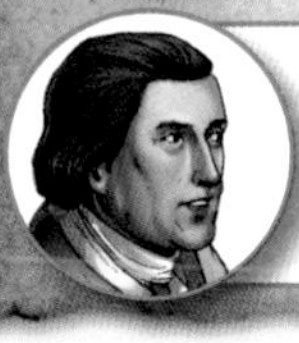

Thomas Jefferson (1743–1826) Writer of the Declaration of Independence, first secretary of state, second vice president, and third president.

The Life of a Colonial Innkeeper

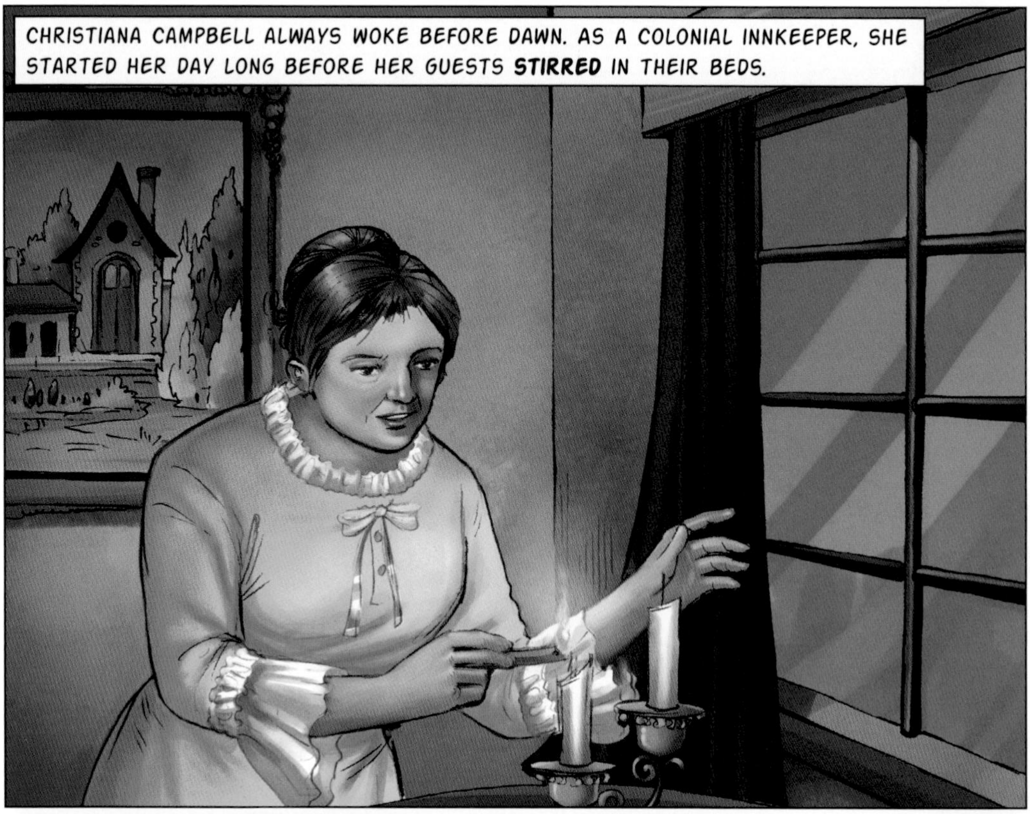
CHRISTIANA CAMPBELL ALWAYS WOKE BEFORE DAWN. AS A COLONIAL INNKEEPER, SHE STARTED HER DAY LONG BEFORE HER GUESTS **STIRRED** IN THEIR BEDS.

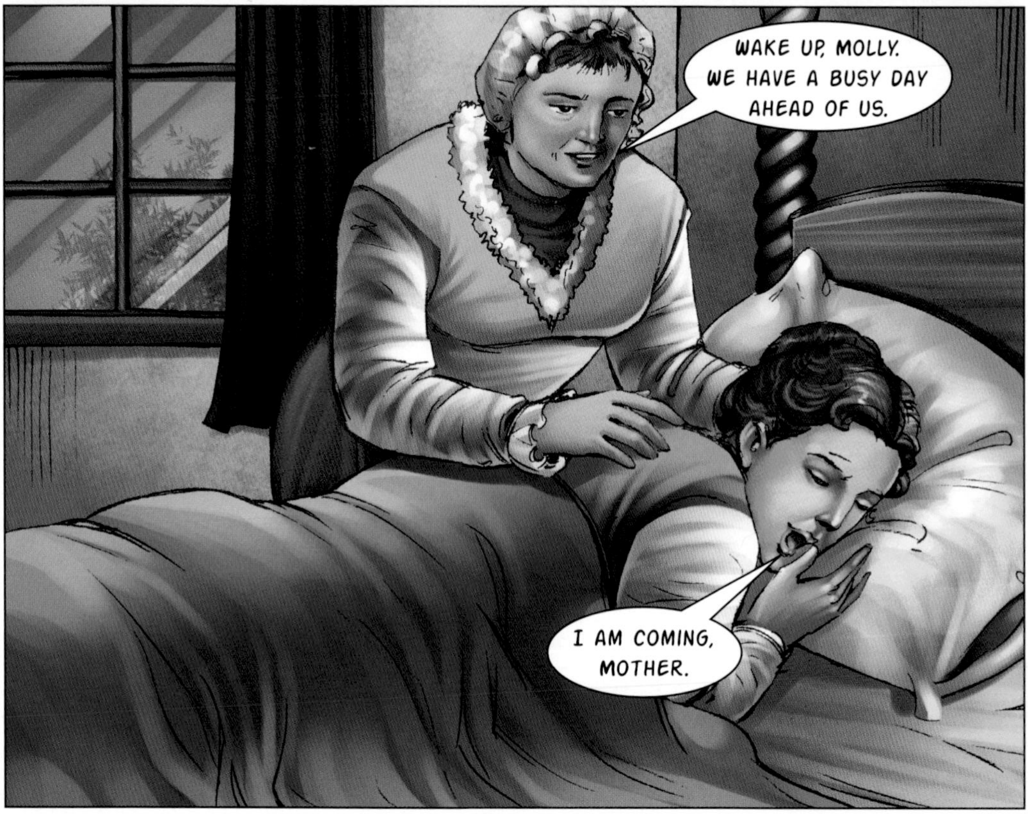
WAKE UP, MOLLY. WE HAVE A BUSY DAY AHEAD OF US.
I AM COMING, MOTHER.

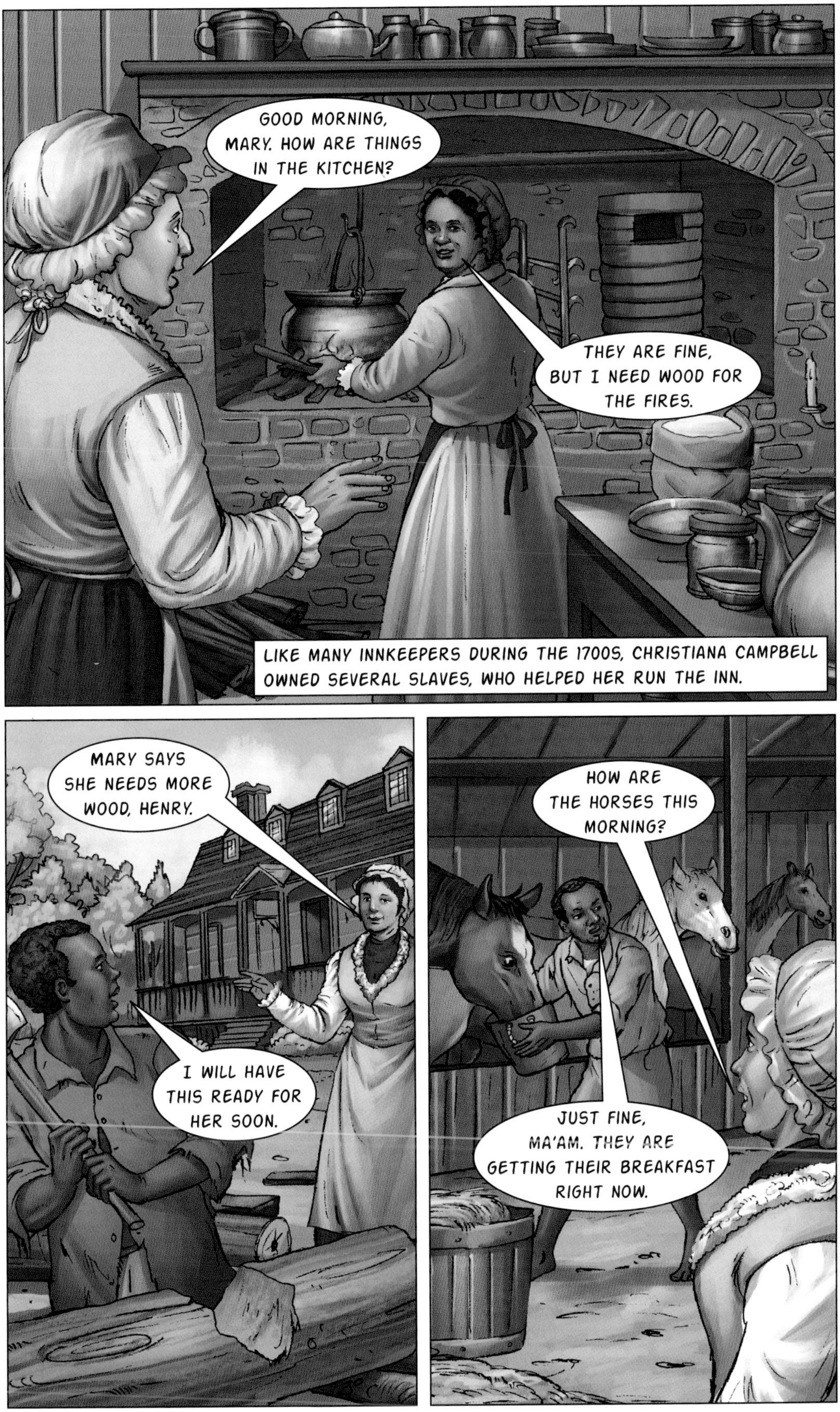
GOOD MORNING, MARY. HOW ARE THINGS IN THE KITCHEN?
THEY ARE FINE, BUT I NEED WOOD FOR THE FIRES.
LIKE MANY INNKEEPERS DURING THE 1700S, CHRISTIANA CAMPBELL OWNED SEVERAL SLAVES, WHO HELPED HER RUN THE INN.
MARY SAYS SHE NEEDS MORE WOOD, HENRY.
I WILL HAVE THIS READY FOR HER SOON.
HOW ARE THE HORSES THIS MORNING?
JUST FINE, MA'AM. THEY ARE GETTING THEIR BREAKFAST RIGHT NOW.

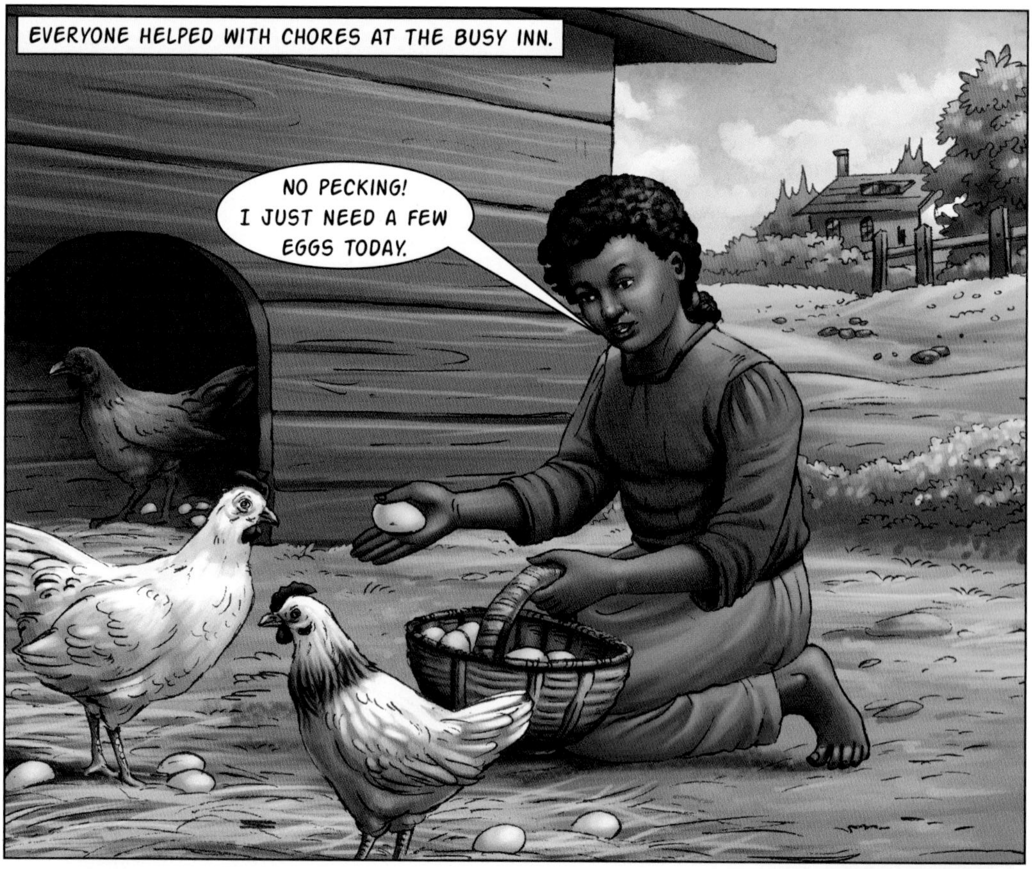
EVERYONE HELPED WITH CHORES AT THE BUSY INN.
NO PECKING! I JUST NEED A FEW EGGS TODAY.

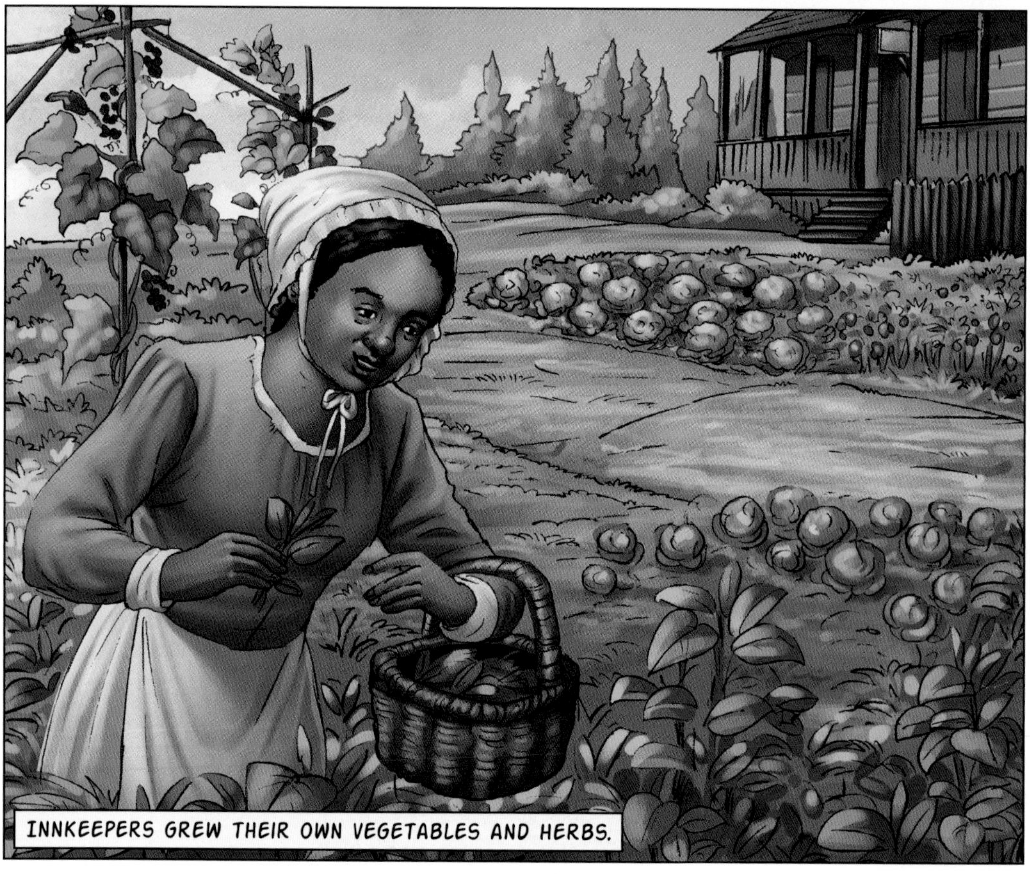
INNKEEPERS GREW THEIR OWN VEGETABLES AND HERBS.

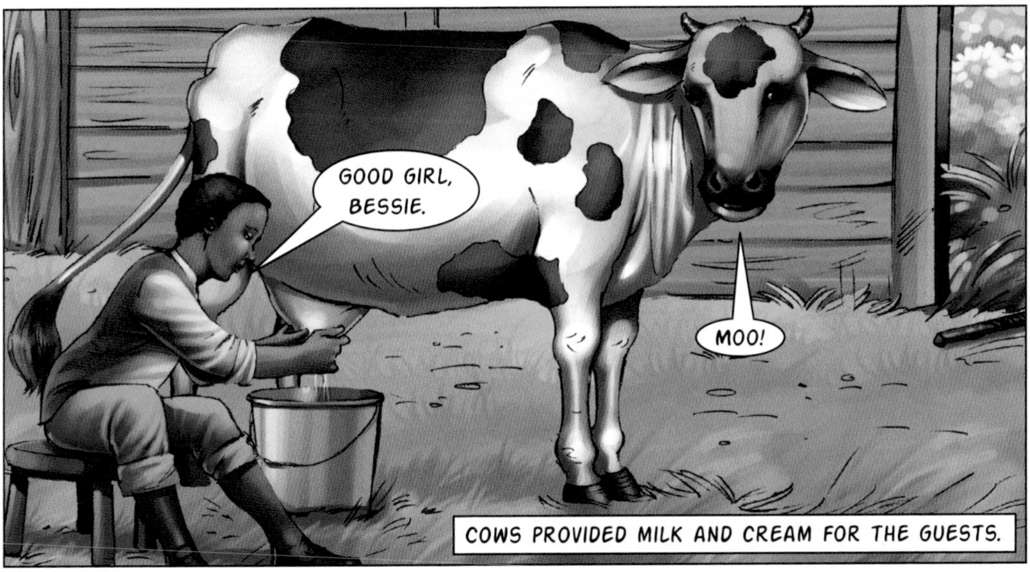
GOOD GIRL, BESSIE.
MOO!
COWS PROVIDED MILK AND CREAM FOR THE GUESTS.

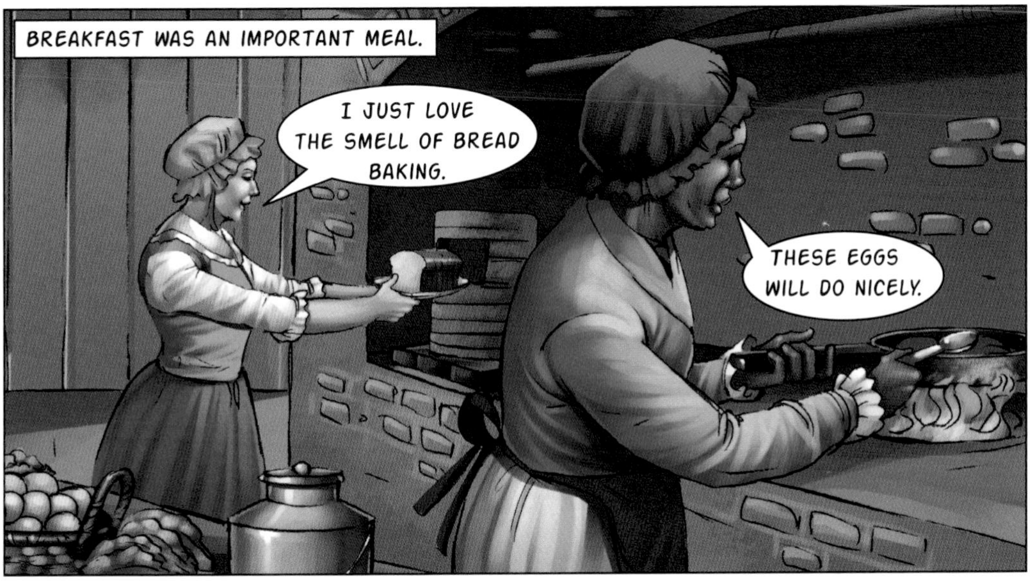
BREAKFAST WAS AN IMPORTANT MEAL.
I JUST LOVE THE SMELL OF BREAD BAKING.
THESE EGGS WILL DO NICELY.

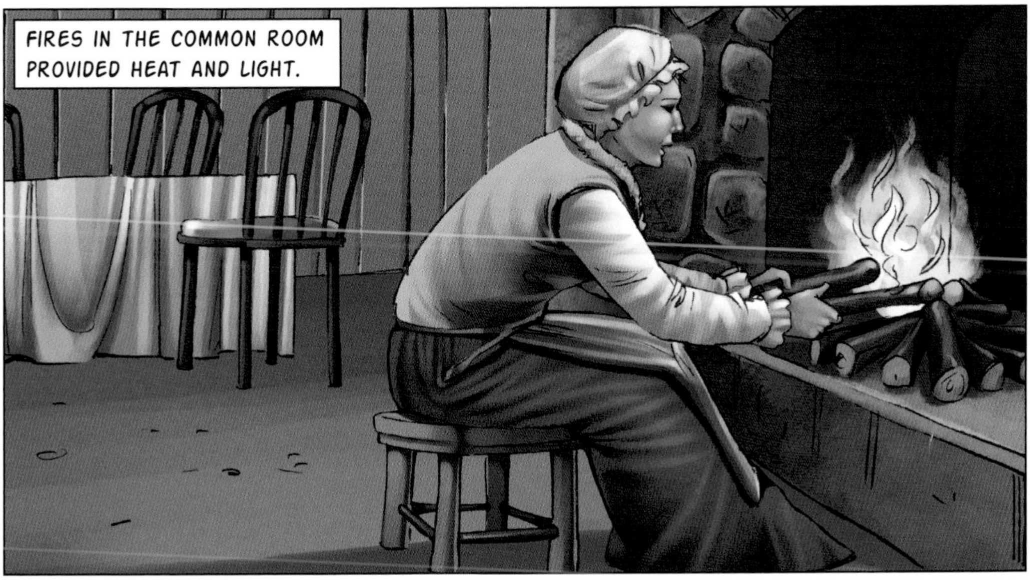
FIRES IN THE COMMON ROOM PROVIDED HEAT AND LIGHT.

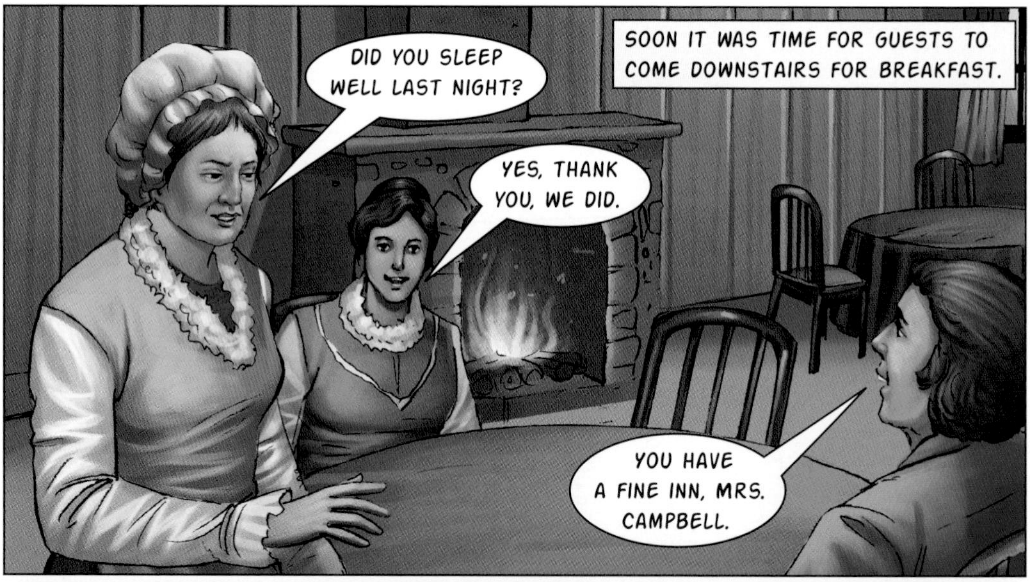
SOON IT WAS TIME FOR GUESTS TO COME DOWNSTAIRS FOR BREAKFAST.
DID YOU SLEEP WELL LAST NIGHT?
YES, THANK YOU, WE DID.
YOU HAVE A FINE INN, MRS. CAMPBELL.

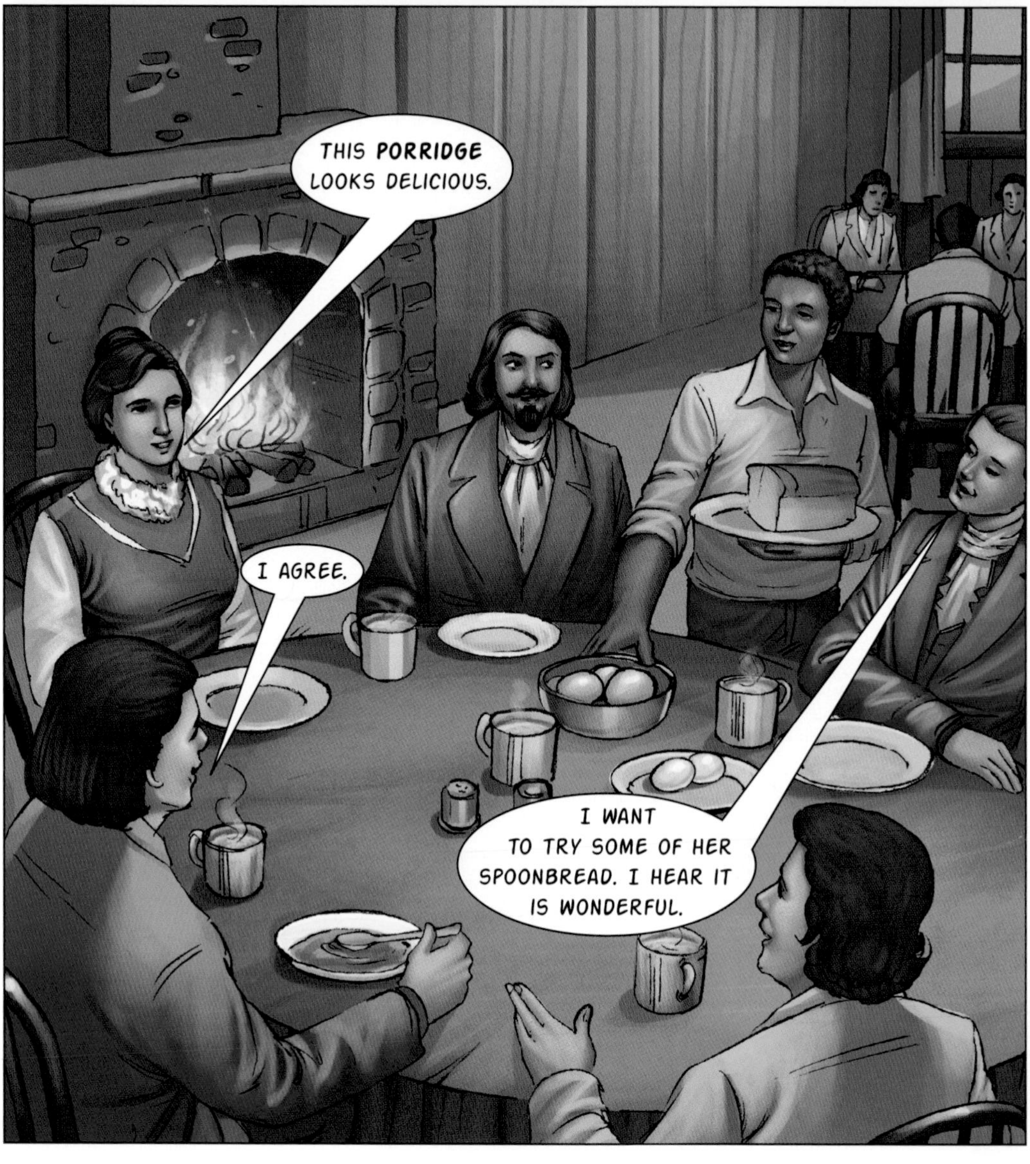
THIS **PORRIDGE** LOOKS DELICIOUS.
I AGREE.
I WANT TO TRY SOME OF HER SPOONBREAD. I HEAR IT IS WONDERFUL.

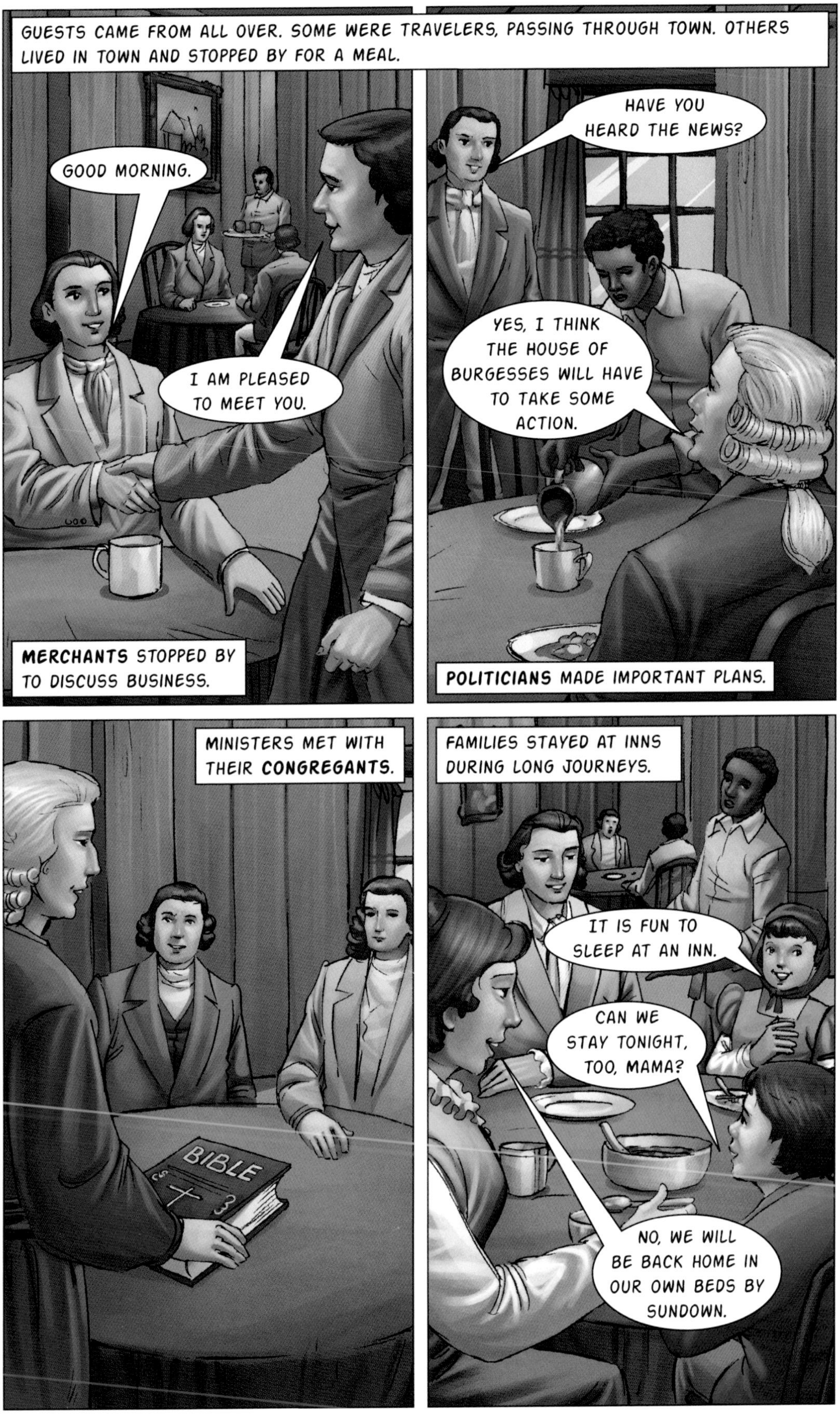
GUESTS CAME FROM ALL OVER. SOME WERE TRAVELERS, PASSING THROUGH TOWN. OTHERS LIVED IN TOWN AND STOPPED BY FOR A MEAL.
GOOD MORNING.
I AM PLEASED TO MEET YOU.
MERCHANTS STOPPED BY TO DISCUSS BUSINESS.
HAVE YOU HEARD THE NEWS?
YES, I THINK THE HOUSE OF BURGESSES WILL HAVE TO TAKE SOME ACTION.
POLITICIANS MADE IMPORTANT PLANS.
MINISTERS MET WITH THEIR CONGREGANTS.
BIBLE
FAMILIES STAYED AT INNS DURING LONG JOURNEYS.
IT IS FUN TO SLEEP AT AN INN.
CAN WE STAY TONIGHT, TOO, MAMA?
NO, WE WILL BE BACK HOME IN OUR OWN BEDS BY SUNDOWN.

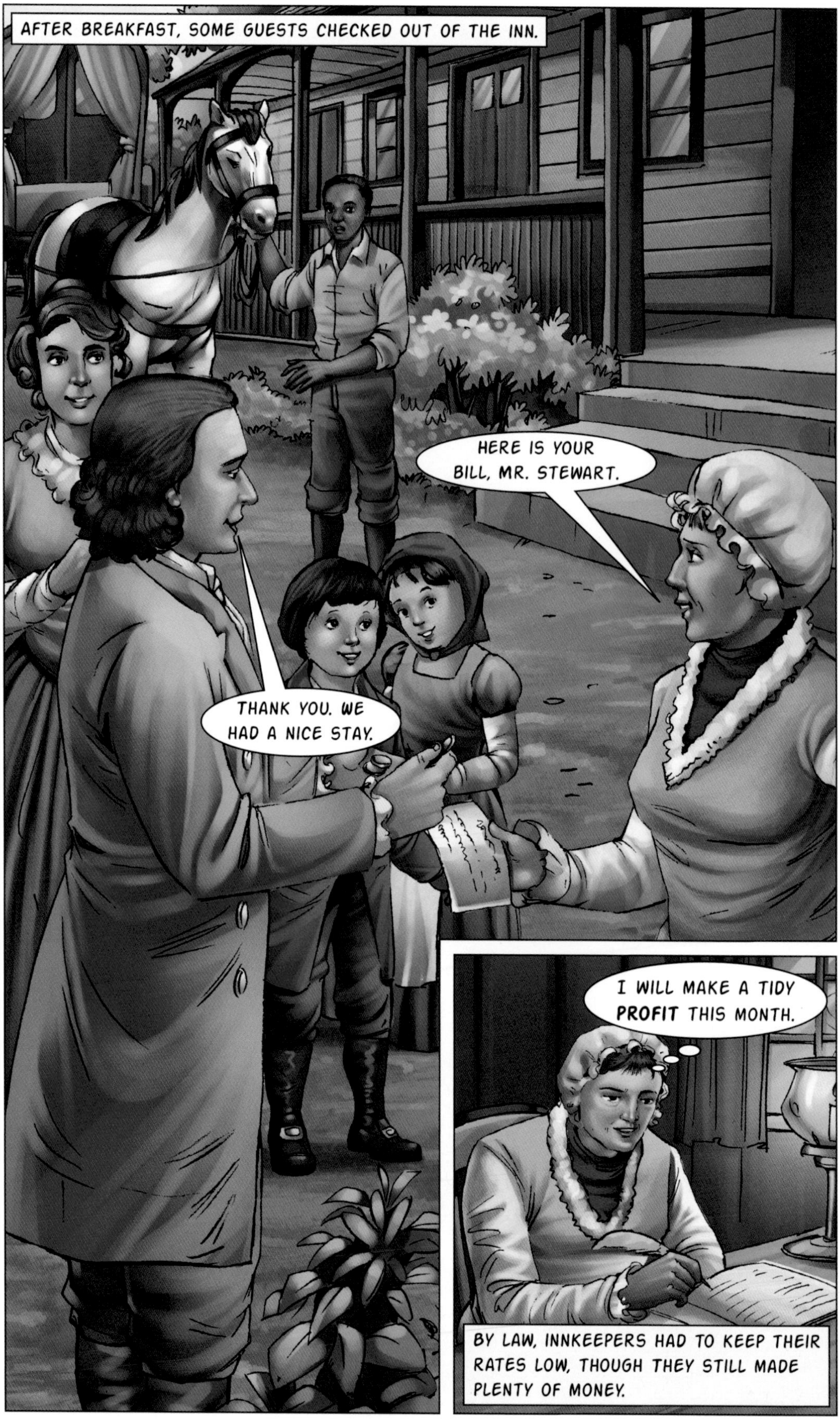
AFTER BREAKFAST, SOME GUESTS CHECKED OUT OF THE INN.
HERE IS YOUR BILL, MR. STEWART.
THANK YOU. WE HAD A NICE STAY.
I WILL MAKE A TIDY **PROFIT** THIS MONTH.
BY LAW, INNKEEPERS HAD TO KEEP THEIR RATES LOW, THOUGH THEY STILL MADE PLENTY OF MONEY.

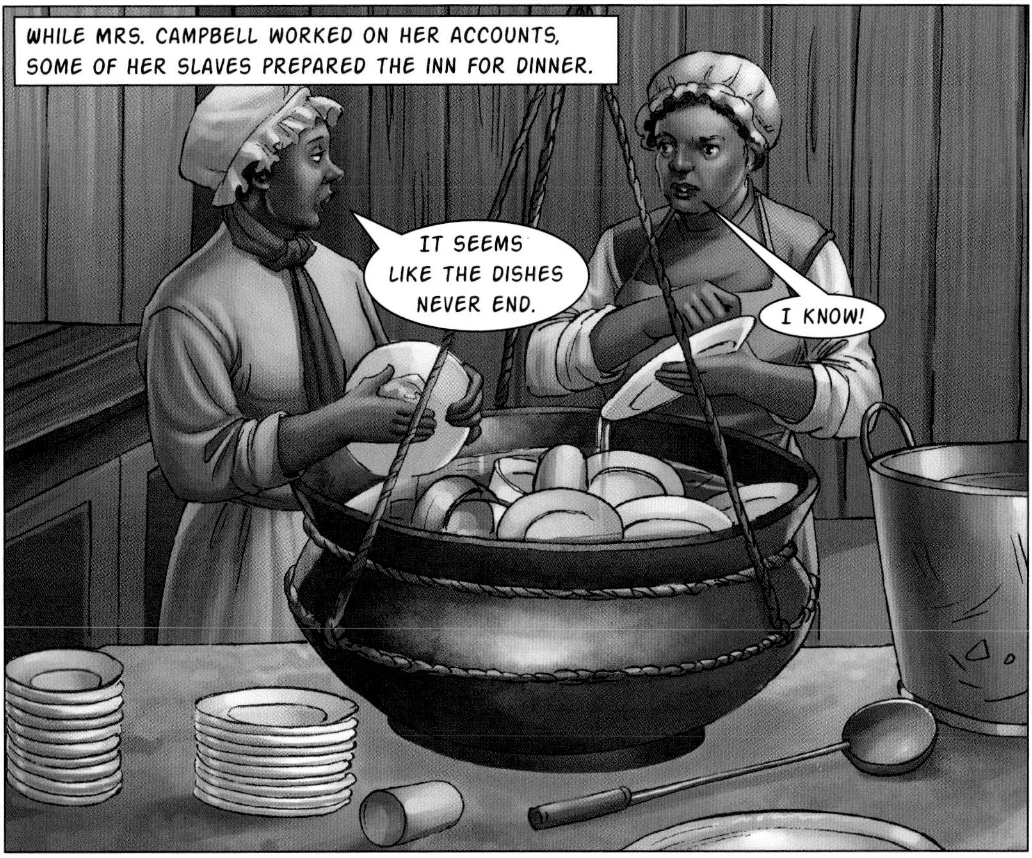
WHILE MRS. CAMPBELL WORKED ON HER ACCOUNTS, SOME OF HER SLAVES PREPARED THE INN FOR DINNER.
IT SEEMS LIKE THE DISHES NEVER END.
I KNOW!

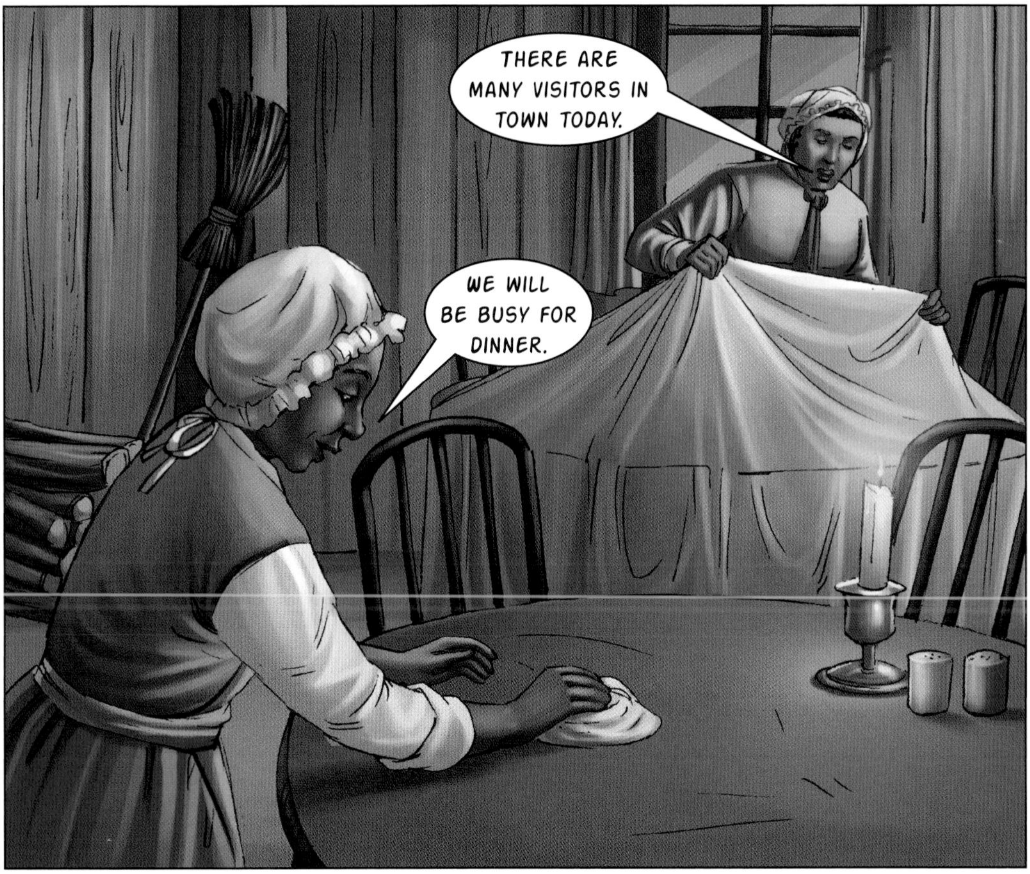
THERE ARE MANY VISITORS IN TOWN TODAY.
WE WILL BE BUSY FOR DINNER.

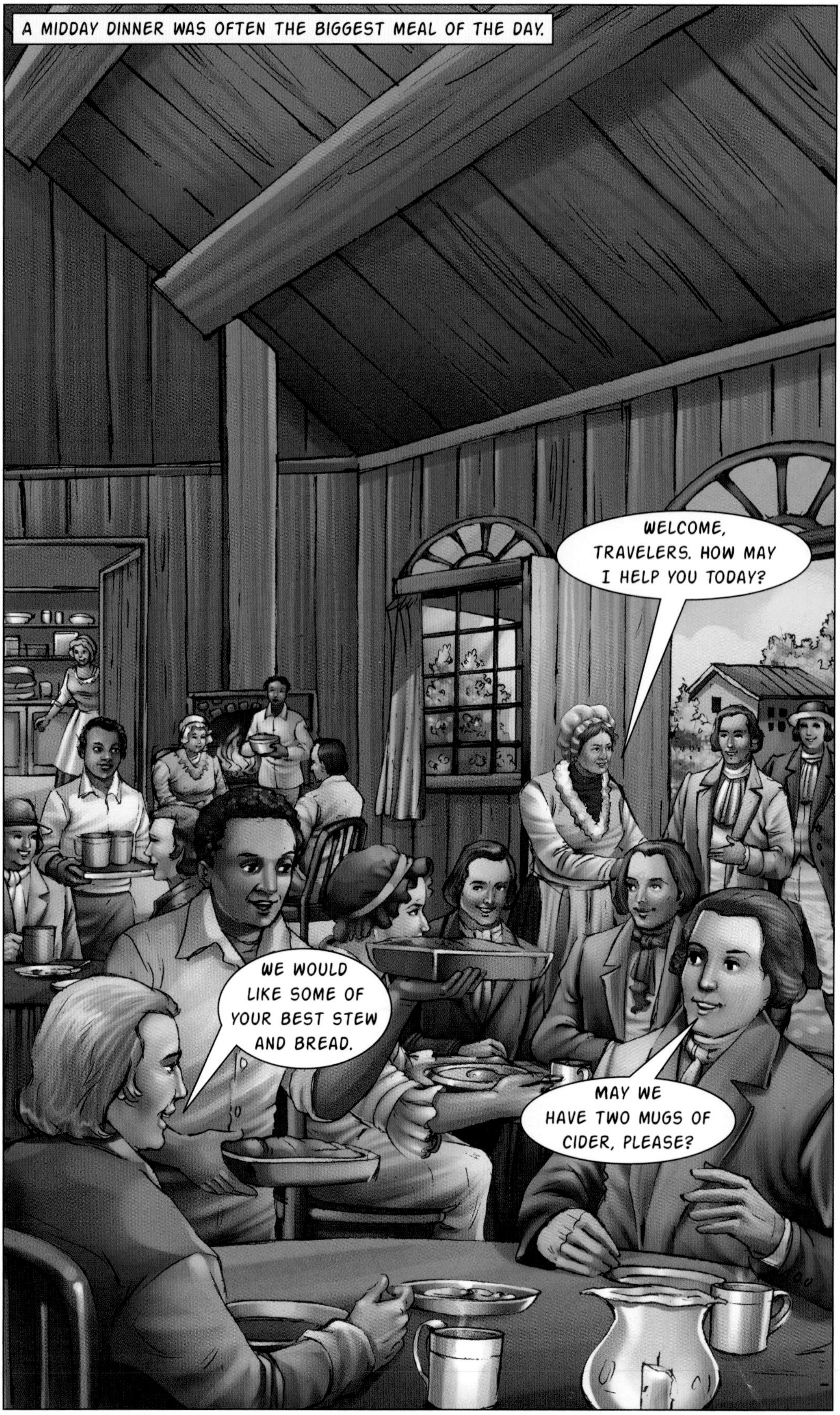
A MIDDAY DINNER WAS OFTEN THE BIGGEST MEAL OF THE DAY.
WELCOME, TRAVELERS. HOW MAY I HELP YOU TODAY?
WE WOULD LIKE SOME OF YOUR BEST STEW AND BREAD.
MAY WE HAVE TWO MUGS OF CIDER, PLEASE?

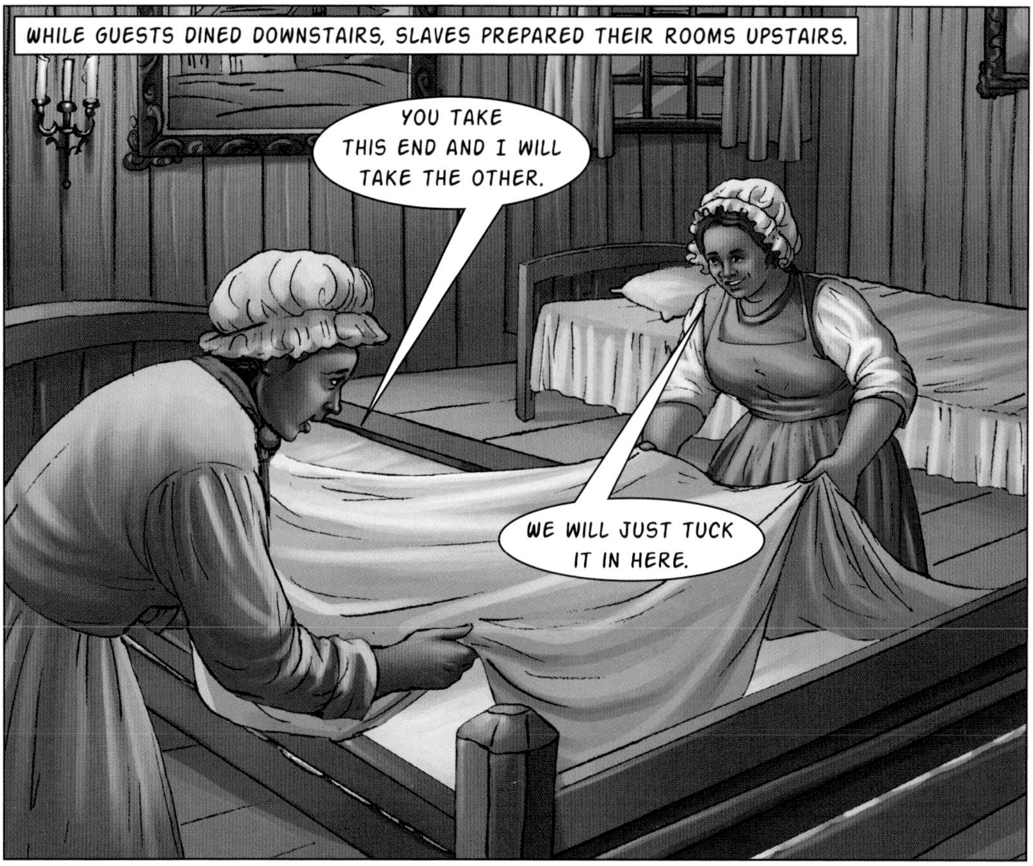
WHILE GUESTS DINED DOWNSTAIRS, SLAVES PREPARED THEIR ROOMS UPSTAIRS.
YOU TAKE THIS END AND I WILL TAKE THE OTHER.
WE WILL JUST TUCK IT IN HERE.

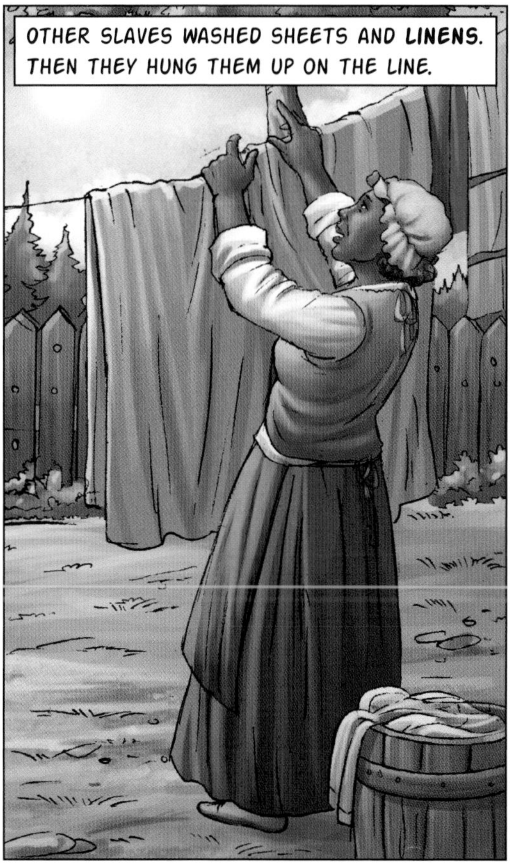
OTHER SLAVES WASHED SHEETS AND **LINENS**. THEN THEY HUNG THEM UP ON THE LINE.

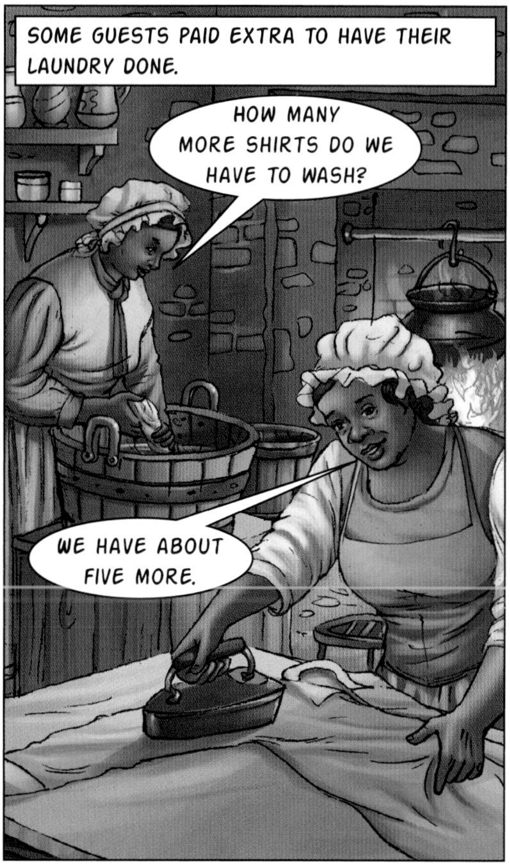
SOME GUESTS PAID EXTRA TO HAVE THEIR LAUNDRY DONE.
HOW MANY MORE SHIRTS DO WE HAVE TO WASH?
WE HAVE ABOUT FIVE MORE.

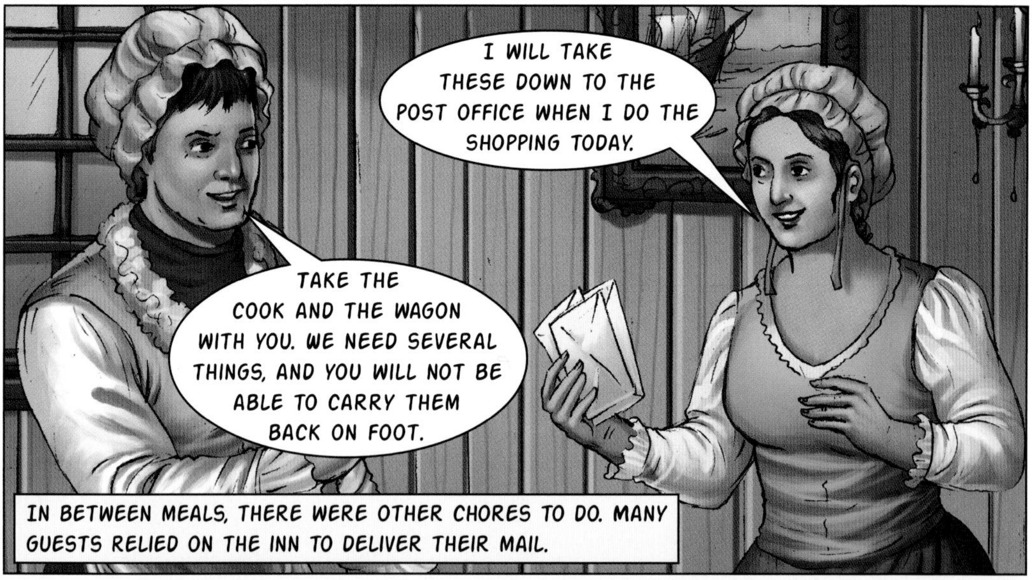
I WILL TAKE THESE DOWN TO THE POST OFFICE WHEN I DO THE SHOPPING TODAY.
TAKE THE COOK AND THE WAGON WITH YOU. WE NEED SEVERAL THINGS, AND YOU WILL NOT BE ABLE TO CARRY THEM BACK ON FOOT.
IN BETWEEN MEALS, THERE WERE OTHER CHORES TO DO. MANY GUESTS RELIED ON THE INN TO DELIVER THEIR MAIL.

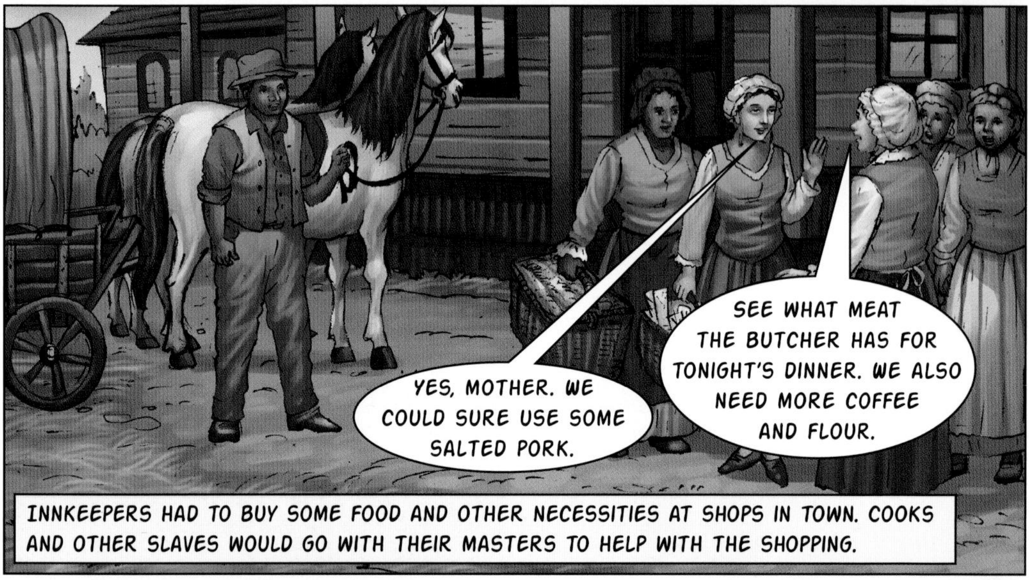
SEE WHAT MEAT THE BUTCHER HAS FOR TONIGHT'S DINNER. WE ALSO NEED MORE COFFEE AND FLOUR.
YES, MOTHER. WE COULD SURE USE SOME SALTED PORK.
INNKEEPERS HAD TO BUY SOME FOOD AND OTHER NECESSITIES AT SHOPS IN TOWN. COOKS AND OTHER SLAVES WOULD GO WITH THEIR MASTERS TO HELP WITH THE SHOPPING.

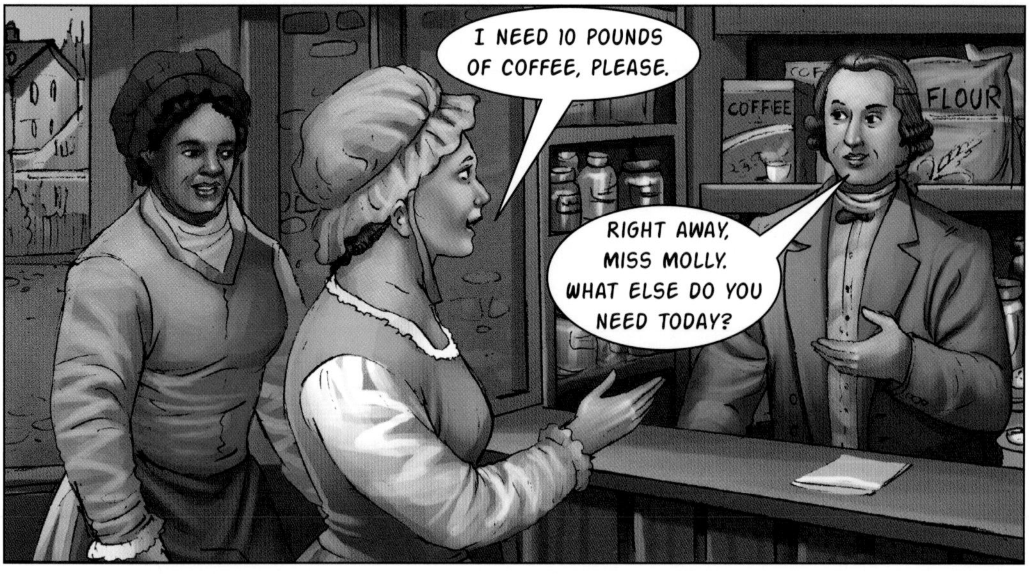
I NEED 10 POUNDS OF COFFEE, PLEASE.
COFFEE
FLOUR
RIGHT AWAY, MISS MOLLY. WHAT ELSE DO YOU NEED TODAY?

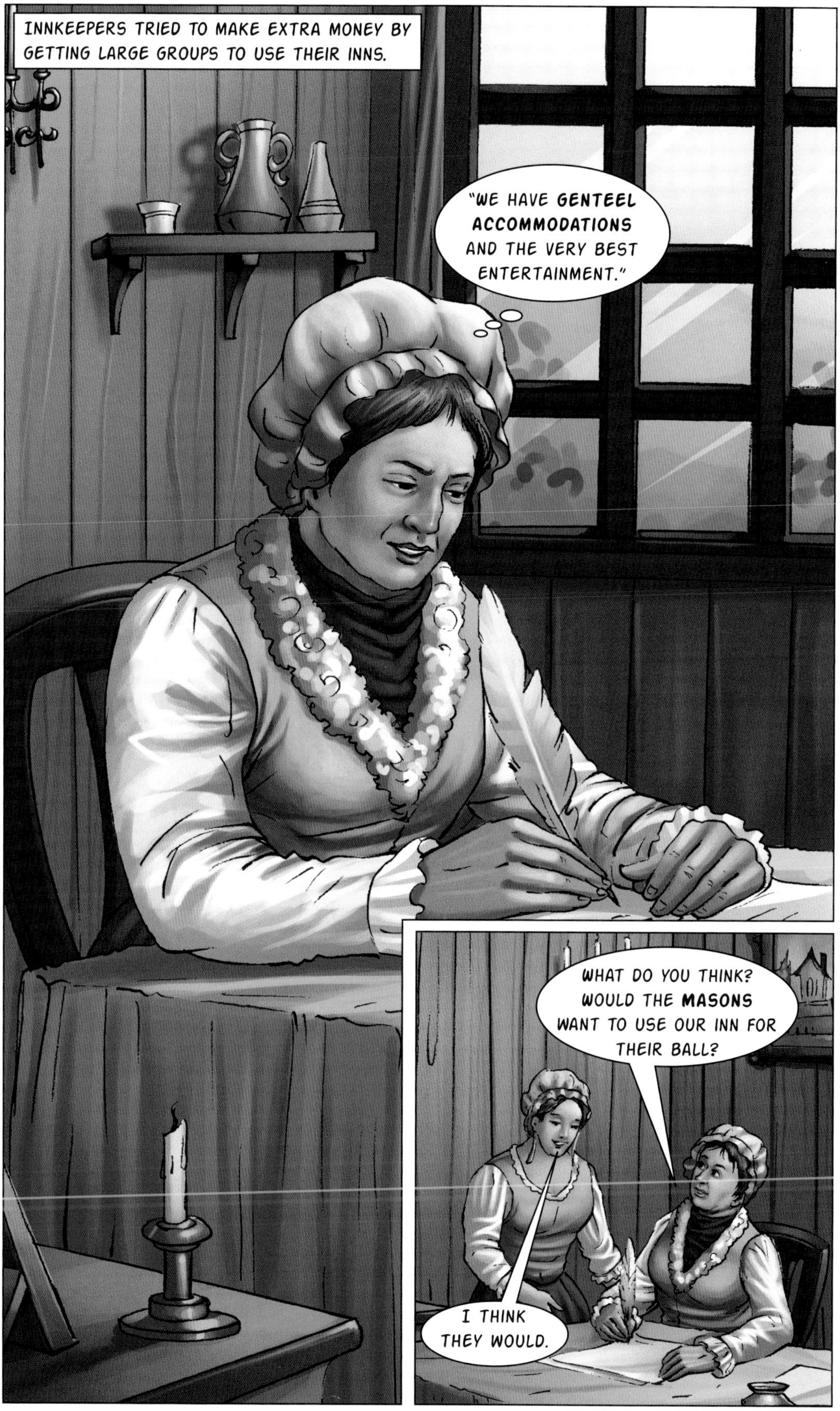
INNKEEPERS TRIED TO MAKE EXTRA MONEY BY GETTING LARGE GROUPS TO USE THEIR INNS.
"WE HAVE **GENTEEL ACCOMMODATIONS** AND THE VERY BEST ENTERTAINMENT."
WHAT DO YOU THINK? WOULD THE **MASONS** WANT TO USE OUR INN FOR THEIR BALL?
I THINK THEY WOULD.

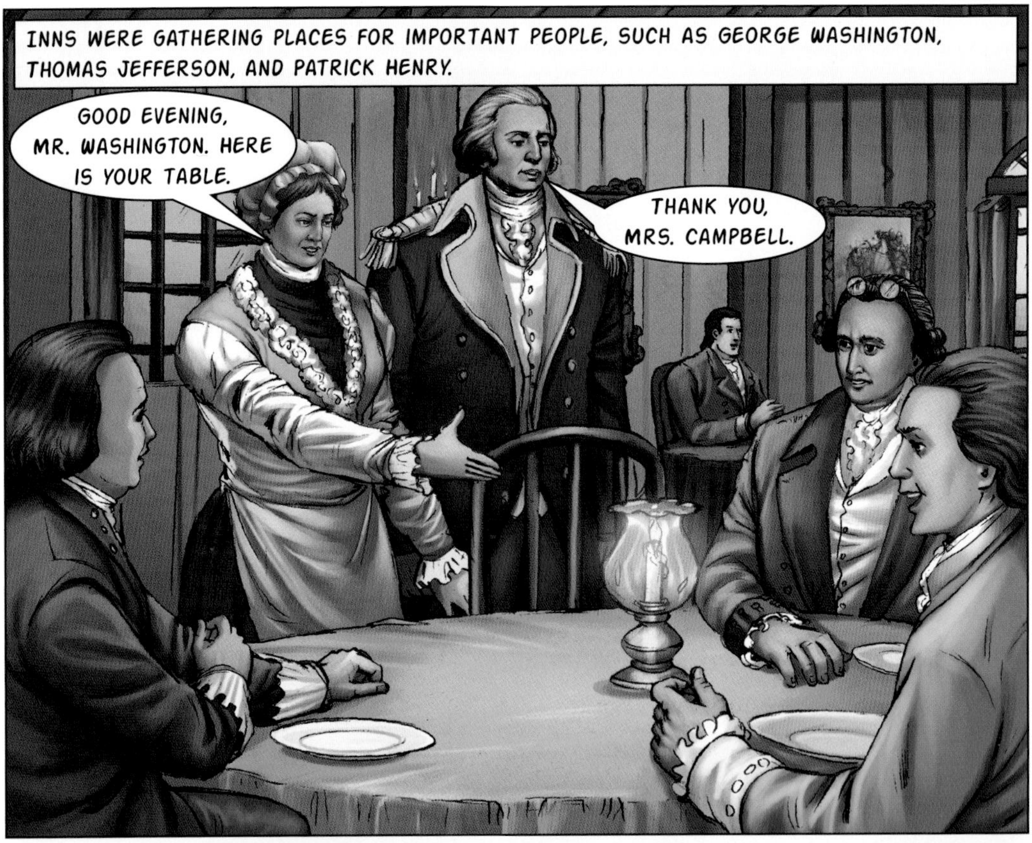
INNS WERE GATHERING PLACES FOR IMPORTANT PEOPLE, SUCH AS GEORGE WASHINGTON, THOMAS JEFFERSON, AND PATRICK HENRY.
GOOD EVENING, MR. WASHINGTON. HERE IS YOUR TABLE.
THANK YOU, MRS. CAMPBELL.

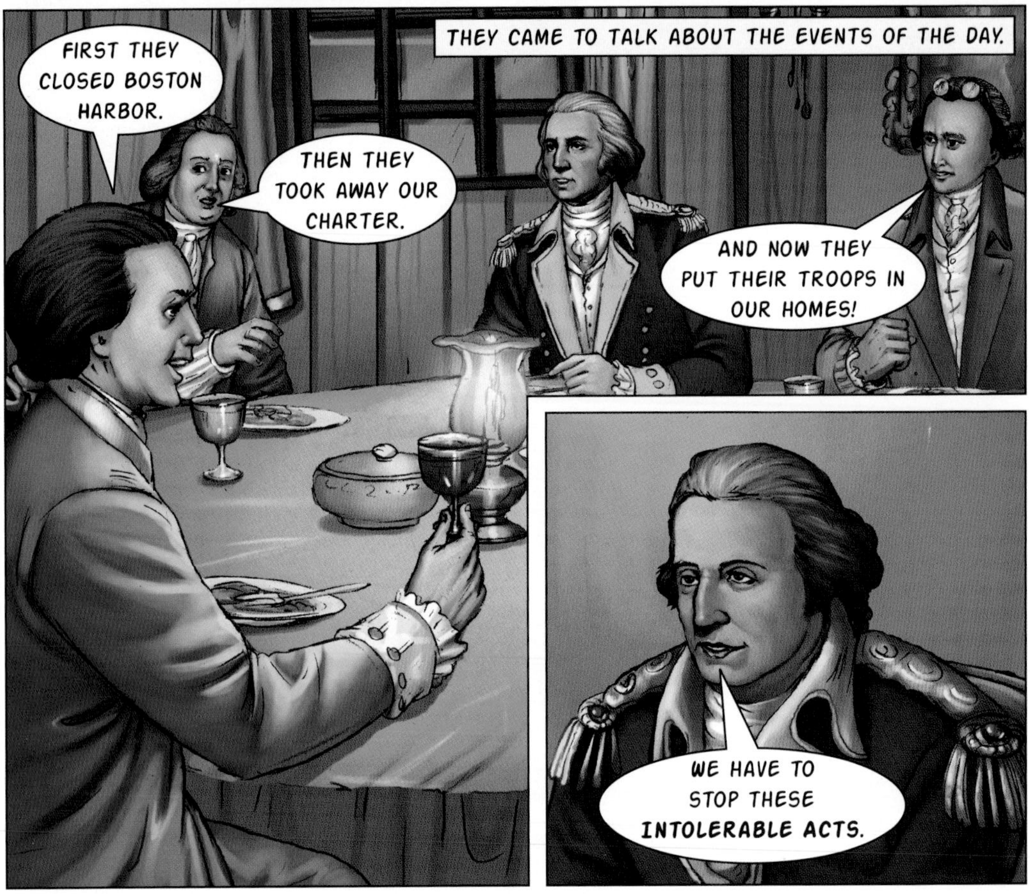
THEY CAME TO TALK ABOUT THE EVENTS OF THE DAY.
FIRST THEY CLOSED BOSTON HARBOR.
THEN THEY TOOK AWAY OUR CHARTER.
AND NOW THEY PUT THEIR TROOPS IN OUR HOMES!
WE HAVE TO STOP THESE **INTOLERABLE ACTS.**

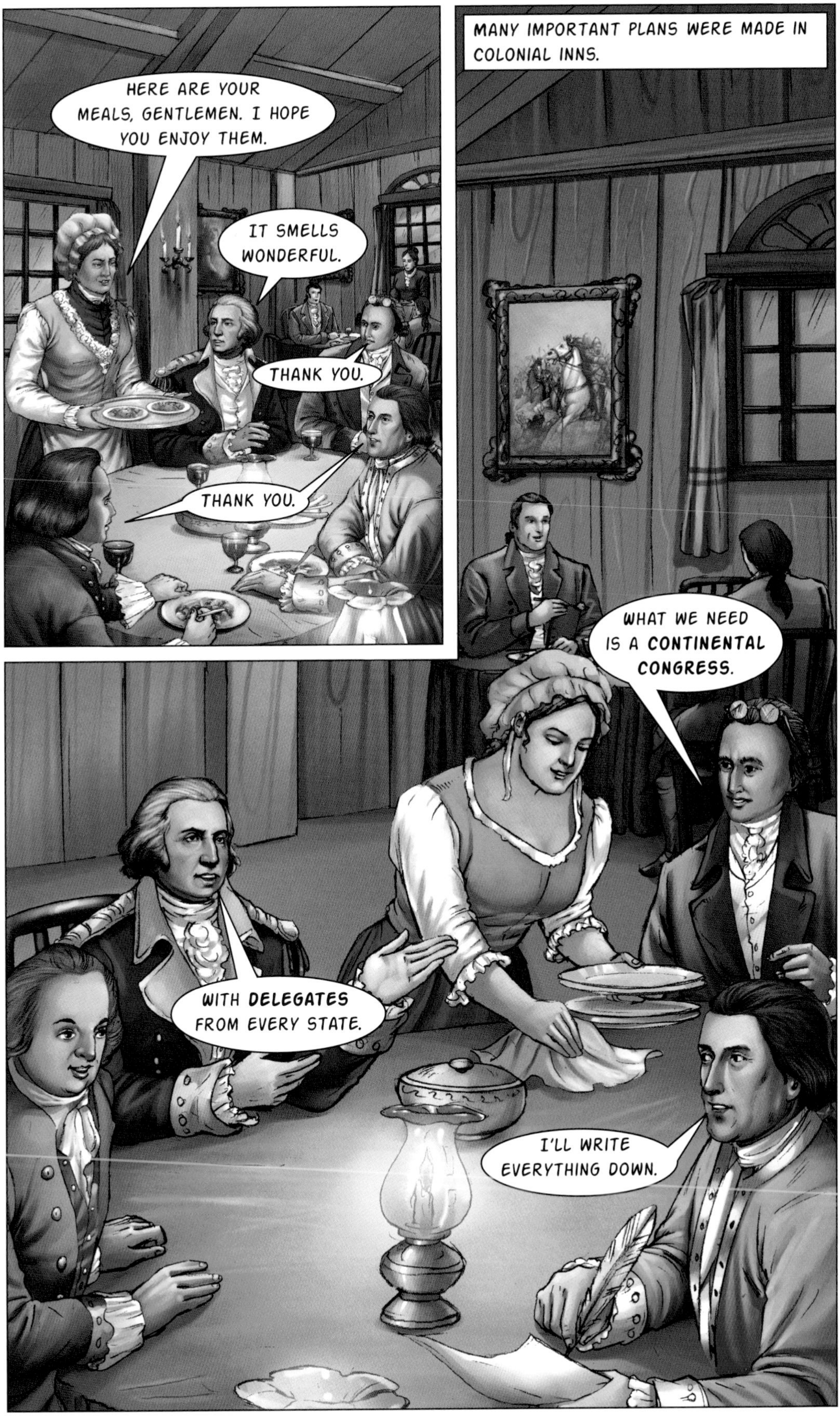
HERE ARE YOUR MEALS, GENTLEMEN. I HOPE YOU ENJOY THEM.
IT SMELLS WONDERFUL.
THANK YOU.
THANK YOU.
MANY IMPORTANT PLANS WERE MADE IN COLONIAL INNS.
WHAT WE NEED IS A **CONTINENTAL CONGRESS.**
WITH **DELEGATES** FROM EVERY STATE.
I'LL WRITE EVERYTHING DOWN.

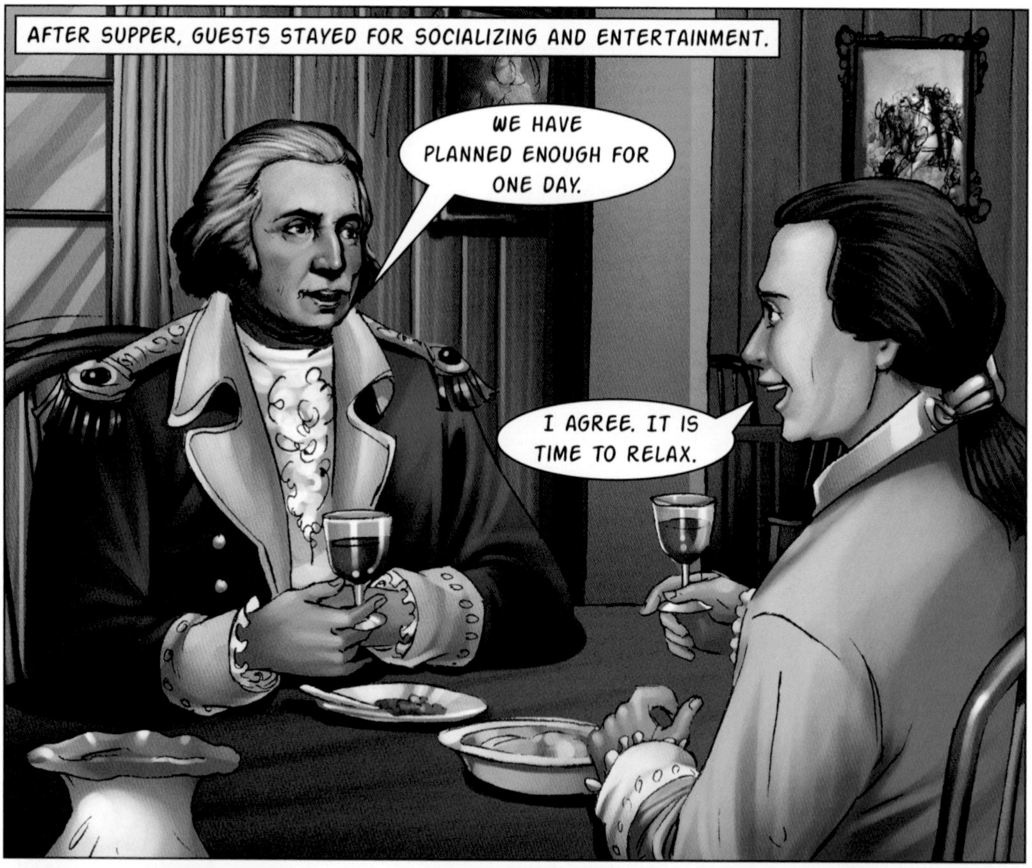
AFTER SUPPER, GUESTS STAYED FOR SOCIALIZING AND ENTERTAINMENT.
WE HAVE PLANNED ENOUGH FOR ONE DAY.
I AGREE. IT IS TIME TO RELAX.

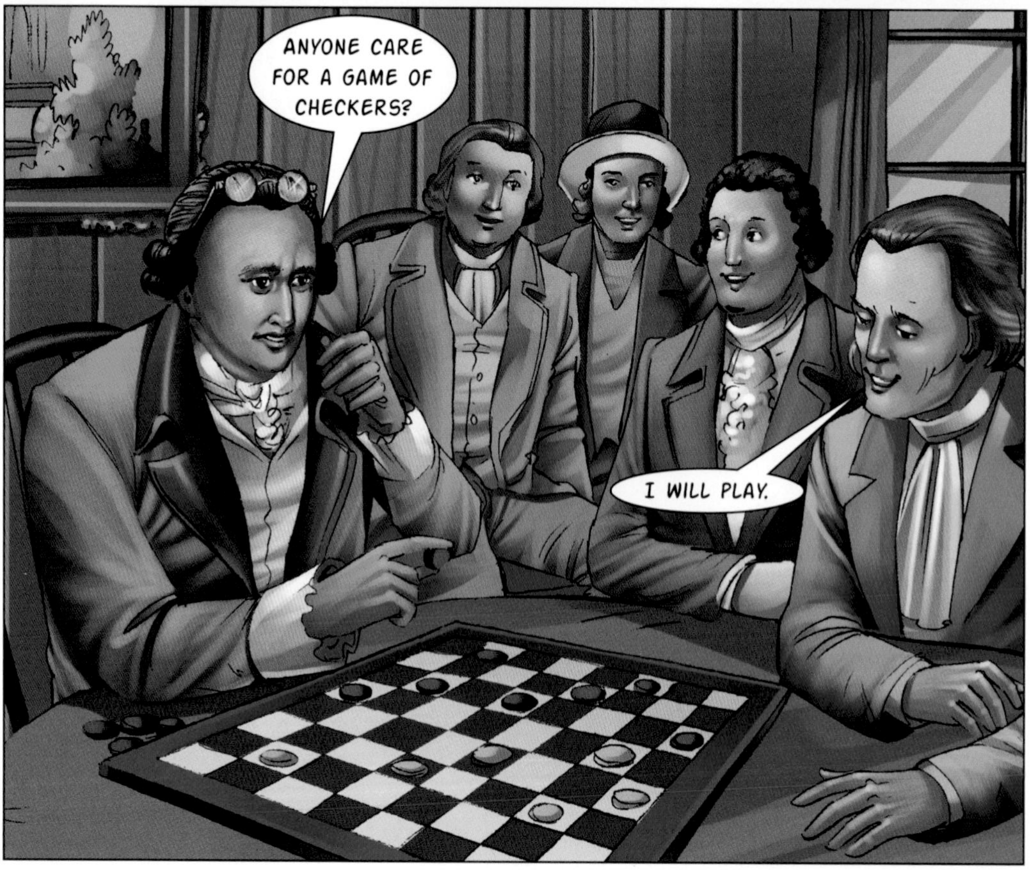
ANYONE CARE FOR A GAME OF CHECKERS?
I WILL PLAY.

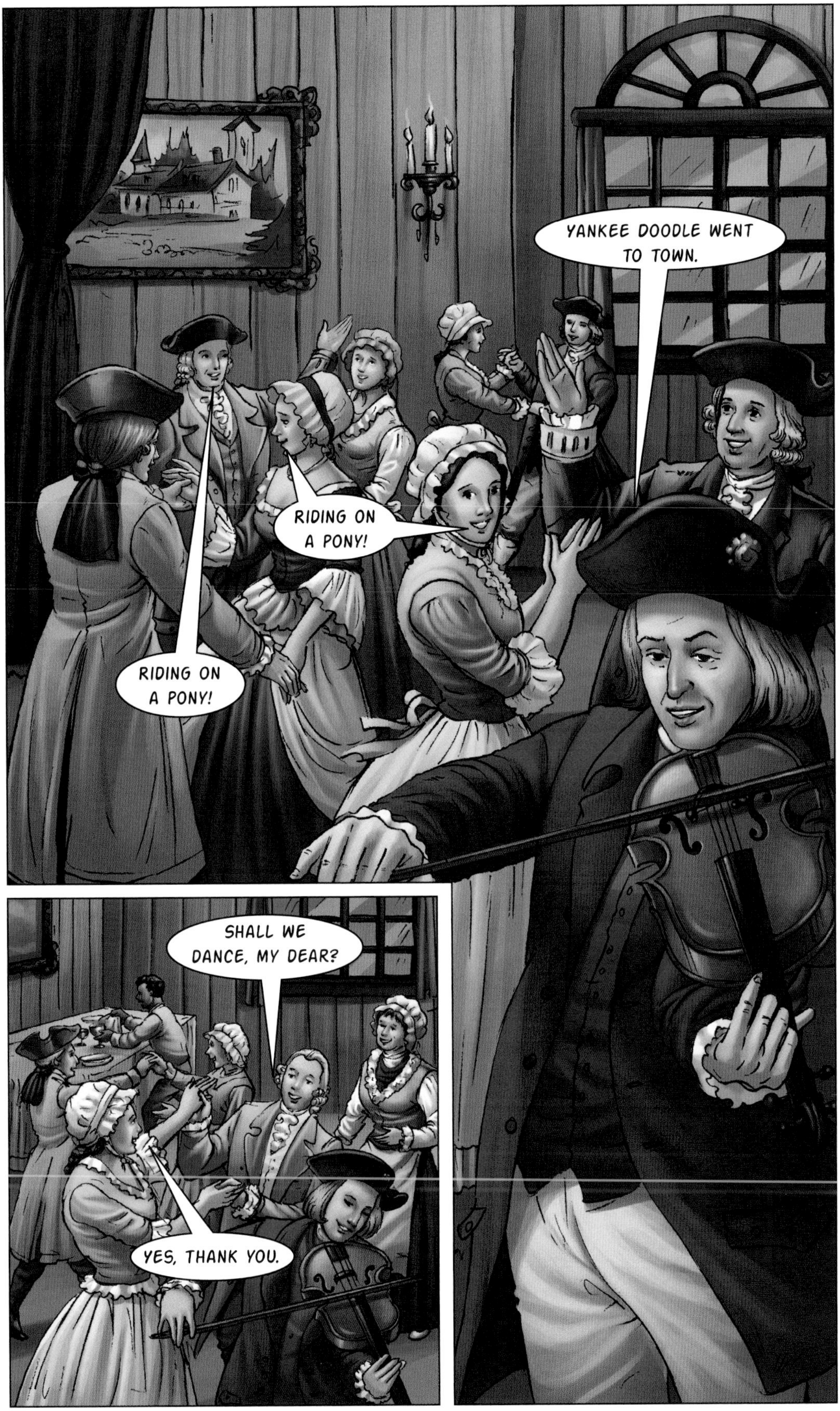
YANKEE DOODLE WENT TO TOWN.
RIDING ON A PONY!
RIDING ON A PONY!
SHALL WE DANCE, MY DEAR?
YES, THANK YOU.

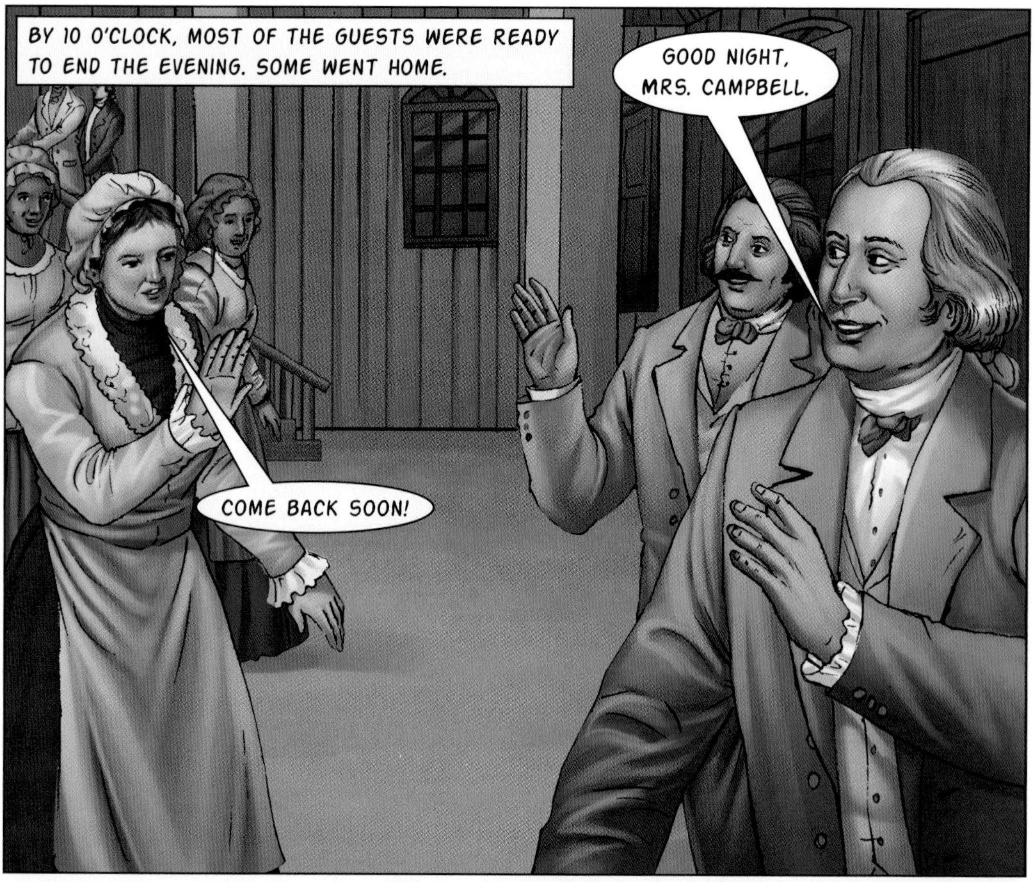
BY 10 O'CLOCK, MOST OF THE GUESTS WERE READY TO END THE EVENING. SOME WENT HOME.
GOOD NIGHT, MRS. CAMPBELL.
COME BACK SOON!

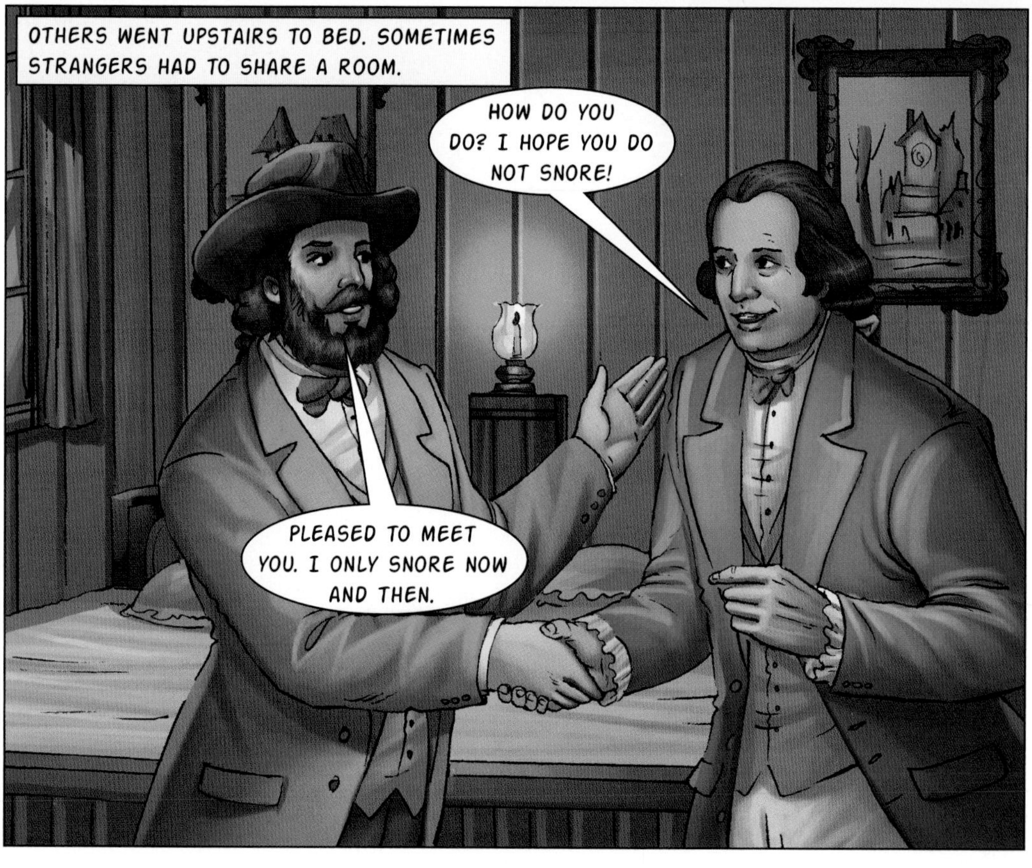
OTHERS WENT UPSTAIRS TO BED. SOMETIMES STRANGERS HAD TO SHARE A ROOM.
HOW DO YOU DO? I HOPE YOU DO NOT SNORE!
PLEASED TO MEET YOU. I ONLY SNORE NOW AND THEN.

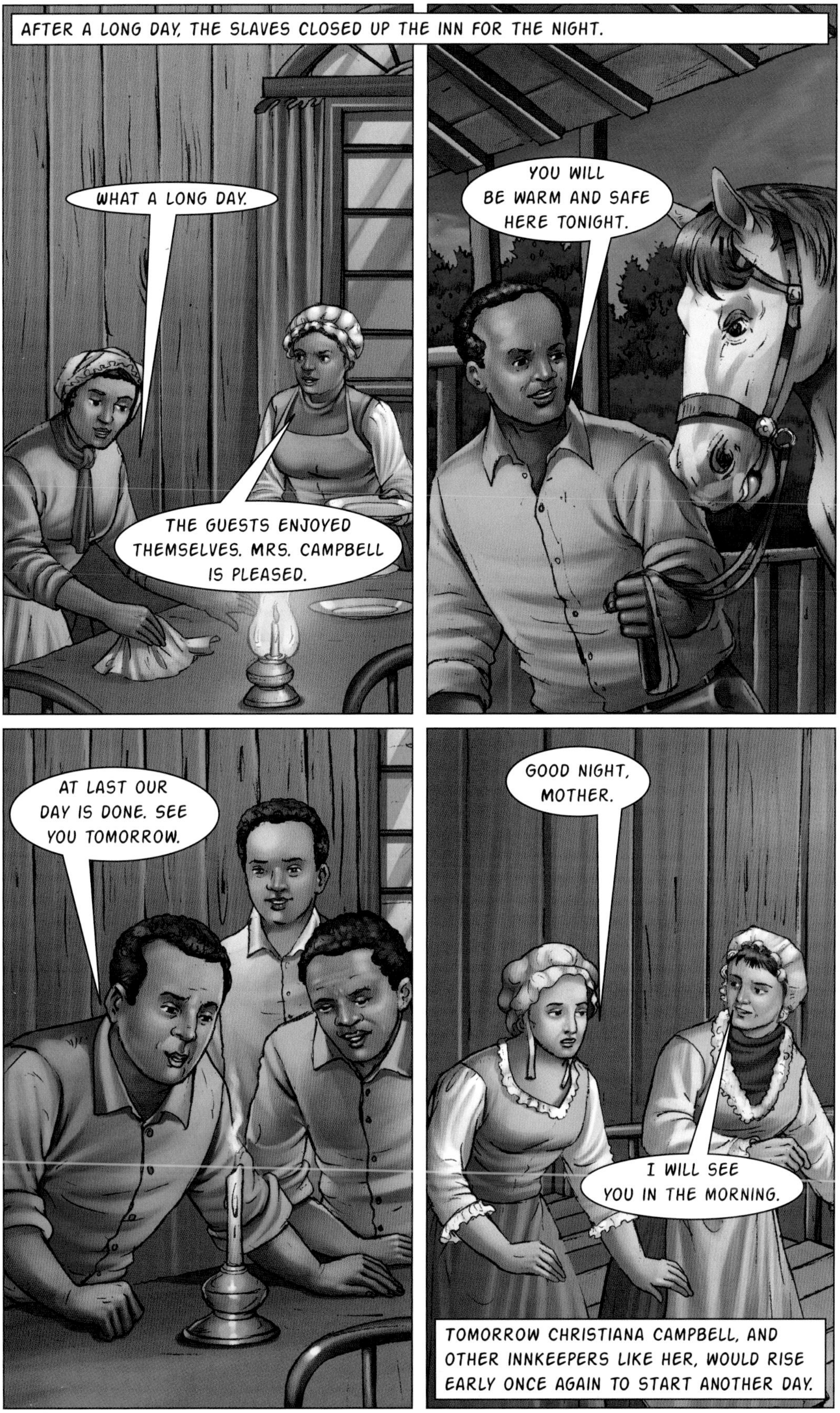
AFTER A LONG DAY, THE SLAVES CLOSED UP THE INN FOR THE NIGHT.
WHAT A LONG DAY.
THE GUESTS ENJOYED THEMSELVES. MRS. CAMPBELL IS PLEASED.
YOU WILL BE WARM AND SAFE HERE TONIGHT.
AT LAST OUR DAY IS DONE. SEE YOU TOMORROW.
GOOD NIGHT, MOTHER.
I WILL SEE YOU IN THE MORNING.
TOMORROW CHRISTIANA CAMPBELL, AND OTHER INNKEEPERS LIKE HER, WOULD RISE EARLY ONCE AGAIN TO START ANOTHER DAY.

Famous Colonial Innkeepers

Samuel "Black Sam" Fraunces
(c. 1722– c. 1795)

Samuel Fraunces moved to New York City from the West Indies in the 1750s. In 1762, he bought the Delancey mansion on the corner of Broad and Pearl streets for 2,000 pounds. After he opened it as a tavern and an inn, it became a popular spot. The Sons of Liberty met there. John Adams stayed at the inn. Members of the Continental Congress liked to dine there. When George Washington became president, he appointed Samuel Fraunces to be the first White House chef.

Eliza Harvey and Ann Harvey
(1600s–1700s)

In 1697, Eliza Harvey's military captain husband was captured by the French. She opened the Harvey Tavern in Portsmouth, New Hampshire, to support her family. The tavern was used for government meetings and as a post office. Soldiers and merchants stayed at the inn. Eliza's daughter-in-law Ann took over the tavern when Eliza died. In the mid-1700s, the tavern housed French prisoners of war and hosted government functions. It also provided food and shelter to the poor.

William Munroe
(1742–1827)

William Munroe, a sergeant and Patriot, ran the Munroe Tavern from 1770 until 1827. The tavern is famous for how it was used after the 1775 Battle of Lexington and Concord. On April 19, 1775, Brigadier General Earl Percy arrived in Lexington with 1,000 troops to aid the retreating British soldiers. He used the Munroe Tavern as headquarters and a field hospital for a short time. In 1789, George Washington visited the tavern after touring the Lexington battle site.

GLOSSARY

accommodations (uh-ko-muh-DAY-shunz) Lodging and meals or traveling space and related services.

congregants (KONG-grih-gunts) Members of a congregation, a group that meets for worship and religious instruction.

Continental Congress (kon-tuh-NEN-tul KON-gres) A group, made up of a few people from every colony, that made decisions for the colonies.

delegates (DEH-lih-gets) Representatives elected to attend a political gathering.

genteel (jen-TEEL) Upper class, stylish, elegant, and free from bad manners.

Intolerable Acts (in-TOL-ruh-bul AKTS) The name the colonists gave to the Coercive Acts.

linens (LIH-nunz) Items such as tablecloths, sheets, or clothing that were usually made of linen.

Masons (MAY-suhnz) Men who belong to a secret society or brotherhood.

merchants (MER-chunts) People who own businesses that sell goods.

politicians (pah-lih-TIH-shunz) People who hold or run for public offices.

porridge (POR-ij) Grain boiled with water until thick and soft, like oatmeal.

profit (PRAH-fit) The money a company makes after all its bills are paid.

stirred (STURD) Began to move, as in awakening.

townsfolk (TOWNZ-fohk) People who live in a town or city.

Harris County Public Library
Houston, Texas

INDEX

WEBSITES

Due to the changing nature of Internet links, PowerKids Press has developed an online list of websites related to the subject of this book. This site is updated regularly. Please use this link to access the list:

www.powerkidslinks.com/jgca/inn/